RAILWAYS AROUND WORCESTERSHIRE

Steve Burdett

AMBERLEY

Acknowledgments and Suggested Reading

My thanks go to Amberley Publishing for allowing me to compose this book.

For those wishing to know more about the area, I can recommend the following publications:

Boynton, J., *The Oxford Worcester and Wolverhampton Railway* (Middle England Books).
Boynton, J., *Rails through the Hills* (Middle England Books).
Great Western Railway Journal, volumes 50 and 54 (Wild Swan Publishing).
Jackson, A., *A Contemporary Perspective on GWR Signalling* (Crowood Press).
Jenkins, S. C., *OWWR Through Time* (Amberley Publishing).
Mitchell, V. and K. Smith, *Western Main Lines: Worcester to Birmingham* (Middleton Press).
Mitchell, V. and K. Smith, *Western Main Lines: Worcester to Hereford* (Middleton Press).

First published 2018

Amberley Publishing
The Hill, Stroud
Gloucestershire, GL5 4EP

www.amberley-books.com

Copyright © Steve Burdett, 2018

The right of Steve Burdett to be identified as the Author of this work has been asserted in accordance with the Copyrights, Designs and Patents Act 1988.

ISBN 978 1 4456 8401 7 (print)
ISBN 978 1 4456 8402 4 (ebook)

British Library Cataloguing in Publication Data.
A catalogue record for this book is available from the British Library.

Origination by Amberley Publishing.
Printed in the UK.

Contents

Introduction

Brought up in North Birmingham and encouraged by my parents, my interest in railways evolved past the normal 'spotting phase', and over the last forty-five years I have recorded my passion both on film and digitally. I do not profess to be a master of the art, and the images included here are more of a record of a changing way of life after the end of steam on British Railways than of an artistic nature.

Worcestershire is very much in the heart of England, and with boundary revisions has seen many changes to its constitutional and physical roles. Once encompassing parts of the Black Country, and even encroaching into the suburbs of Birmingham, it now possesses a more distinct character away from the heavy industry that was to be found in Dudley and surrounding areas. Worcester is a popular vibrant cathedral city, and quite rightly the administrative centre for the county is situated on the banks of the country's longest river, the Severn. Other large centres include Kidderminster, once a major centre for the carpet industry, Redditch, a centre for needle manufacturing, and the Malverns, dominated by those elegant hills. We should not forget the Vale of Evesham, which is arguably the Garden of England.

In common with the rest of the United Kingdom, the county's railways have seen many changes over the last fifty years, and while the Beeching Axe was effective in seeing many rural branch lines removed from the network, the remainder have survived and are now undergoing a minor transformation. With its extensive locomotive works and depots, at one time Worcester saw many main-line services calling there on routes between Birmingham, Bristol, Cardiff, Hereford and London Paddington. However, due to its geographical position and a craving to reduce journey times, direct trains between Birmingham and Bristol frustratingly miss the city, with intending passengers being forced to use connecting services at Cheltenham Spa. Cotswold line trains have seen a resurgence in frequency, and with the redoubling of sections of the route, the future looks good. A new Parkway station is being constructed at Norton, which when completed should see the travelling habits of Worcester folk change dramatically. However, as with all such projects, there remain many issues to be resolved, to which I will refer later.

To the north-east of the county are Bromsgrove and Redditch, both of which will benefit from revised CrossCity line services. Both suffered from sparse services from Birmingham in the 1970s but Redditch now has a healthy service. Bromsgrove will benefit following the construction of a new four-platform station, which will see a number of services that presently terminate at Longbridge being extended there. Electrification of the Lickey Incline will enable this improvement and it is anticipated that certain other cross-country services will call there. However, there remains an element of doubt as to whether a full service will be possible given the relative close proximity of the evolving Worcester Parkway development.

To the west of the county, services over the northern section of the old Oxford Worcester & Wolverhampton Railway (OWWR) are also buoyant towards Kidderminster, Stourbridge and Birmingham Snow Hill. The new West Midlands Railway franchise is committed to increased services and rolling stock, which once again will benefit the good folk of Worcester, who are already seeing new trains on the Cotswold route.

It will be noticeable within the images in this book that I have dwelled upon a dwindling aspect of the railway scene. Worcester and its immediate environs is still in the main controlled by mechanical signalling, which is something that most people tend to associate with preserved railways. How much longer this way of life will continue is unsure, but I hope that these pages will encourage enthusiasts and people with an interest in transport history to visit the area.

I have tried to include a variety of images of motive power that can or have been observed in the area, whether steam or diesel, on regular or special workings.

I do not intend the book to be an historical tome, but rather to contribute to the rich transport tapestry of our lovely country. I have included relevant dates within the captions and any observations are of a purely personal opinion.

The Grade II listed bridge over the A38 at Foregate Street dates back to 1860. It was the subject of major repairs in 2012. Note the GWR shield flanked by two city shields. 11 February 2015.

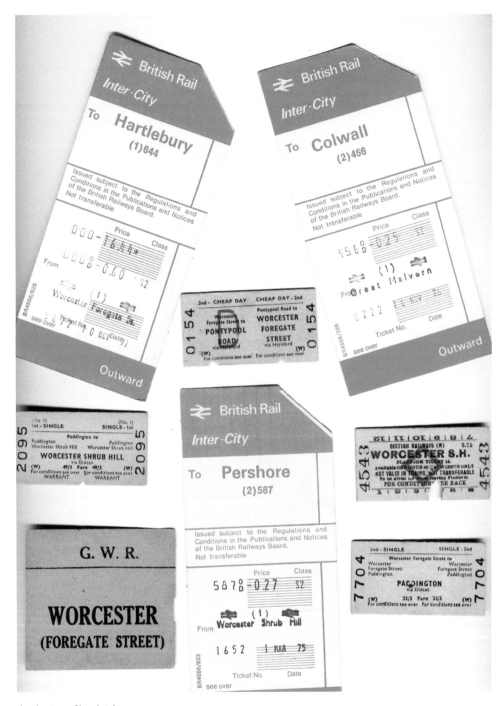

A selection of local tickets.

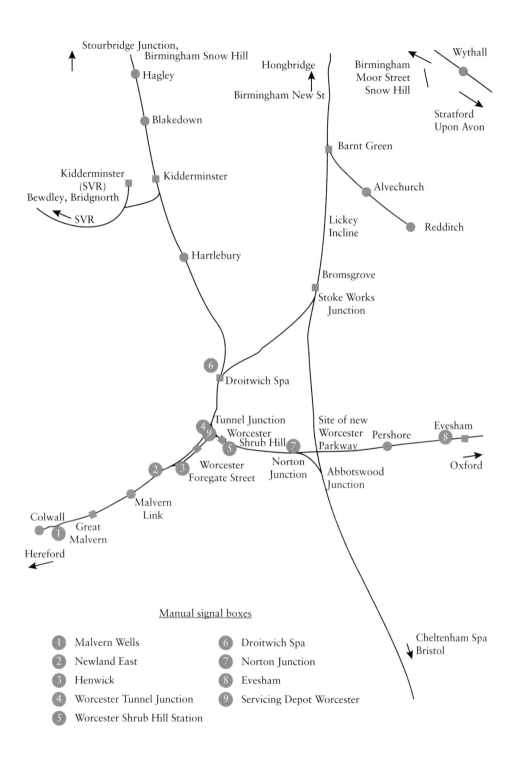

Stourbridge Junction,
Birmingham Snow Hill

Hongbridge

Birmingham
Moor Street
Snow Hill

Wythall

Hagley

Birmingham New St

Stratford
Upon Avon

Blakedown

Barnt Green

Kidderminster
(SVR)
Bewdley, Bridgnorth

Kidderminster

Alvechurch

SVR

Redditch

Lickey
Incline

Hartlebury

Bromsgrove

Stoke Works
Junction

6

Droitwich Spa

Tunnel Junction
Worcester
Shrub Hill

Site of new
Worcester
Parkway

Pershore

Evesham

4
9

8

5

7

Worcester
Foregate Street

Norton
Junction

Oxford

2
3

Abbotswood
Junction

Malvern
Link

Colwall

Great
Malvern

1

Hereford

Cheltenham Spa
Bristol

Manual signal boxes

1 Malvern Wells
2 Newland East
3 Henwick
4 Worcester Tunnel Junction
5 Worcester Shrub Hill Station

6 Droitwich Spa
7 Norton Junction
8 Evesham
9 Servicing Depot Worcester

Worcester Foregate Street
(122 miles from London Paddington)

The Great Western Railway has long held a reputation for siting its stations some distance from the place intended to be served. However, it bucked the trend in 1860 when it sited Foregate Street station in Worcester city centre. Constructed on brick arches, it has to be one of the most convenient stations on its network. It is not without fault and its cramped site leading out towards the River Severn can provide a busy and confusing series of operations for a passenger base in excess of two million per annum.

The track layout was altered in 1973 and trains run in a bidirectional manner, which can be confusing to the travelling public. While there are only two platforms, the stairs from street level can be intimidating should the lifts be out of action. Looking to the west it is hard to imagine that a short branch line dropped down to the river level, which must have been a boon to racehorse owners who chose to move their steeds by rail to the nearby course.

Despite its size, the station serves a number of interesting destinations. Great Western Railway provides services to London Paddington, Hereford, Weymouth, Southampton and even Brighton (the latter via Bristol Temple Meads). Meanwhile, West Midlands Trains serve Birmingham New Street, Snow Hill, Stratford-upon-Avon and Leamington Spa. Occasional charter trains visit the station but due to short platform lengths the preferred station in Worcester is at Shrub Hill.

An occasional treat can be the sight of a steam locomotive using a triangular movement via Henwick to run round charter trains terminating at Shrub Hill.

Westward trains head towards Hereford by way of a 935-yard bridge over the River Severn, which affords splendid views of Worcester Cathedral and the city.

A Class 118 diesel multiple unit (DMU) calls at Worcester Foregate Street on a service from Hereford to Worcester Shrub Hill. A year later, the lines through the station were converted to bidirectional working. 17 June 1972.

Three minutes after leaving Worcester Shrub Hill, High Speed Train (HST) power car No. 43140 enters Worcester Foregate Street with a London Paddington to Hereford service. These iconic InterCity 125 trains are gradually being replaced on these services by new Hitachi IETs. 8 March 2011.

It is rare to witness freight trains passing Worcester Foregate Street, but on 18 August 2016 services were affected by engineering work. This is the Margam to Round Oak steel train, which was diverted via Hereford and Great Malvern. It is seen passing the café on Platform 1, which used to house a signal cabin. The locomotive is General Motors No. 66126.

A series of steam charters regularly visit the city. Most services terminate at Shrub Hill, but require the locomotive to turn by way of a movement through Foregate Street and Henwick. New-build A1 Pacific No. 60163 *Tornado* is captured during such a movement, having worked a Steam Dreams 'Cathedrals Express' from Tonbridge on 19 March 2013.

West Country Pacific No. 34046 *Braunton* requires no turning as it calls at Foregate Street on the Railway Touring Company's 'Welsh Borders Express', which was a circular tour from Bristol Temple Meads via Abergavenny and Hereford. 17 May 2014.

Diesel workings apart from departmental, charter and diverted freights are rare at Foregate Street. The Class 40 Preservation Society's No. 40145 *East Lancashire Railway* makes a rare visit with Pathfinders Tours' 'The Torbay Whistler', running from Tame Bridge Parkway to Kingswear via Hereford, on 20 September 2008. No. 40145 entered traffic in 1961.

A couple of eager enthusiasts record English Electric loco No. 37057 on a test train, working from Derby to Cardiff Canton and approaching Foregate Street, from where, having reached Henwick, it will return on the near track for Shrub Hill. The locomotive was built in 1962 and is now owned by Colas Rail Freight. 15 August 2016.

The Class 150 Sprinters have been a regular sight at Foregate Street for the best part of thirty years, and while many were transferred from London Midland, they continue to be seen on GWR and occasionally on West Midlands services between Hereford and Birmingham New Street, as with No. 150105, which is seen on 24 July 2012.

Class 170 Turbos are the usual motive power for Hereford services from New Street. The 17.49 from New Street has just called at Shrub Hill before leaving Foregate Street for Hereford on 2 February 2017.

Leaving Foregate Street, trains traverse a 935-yard bridge comprising sixty-eight brick arches, lattice girders and an embankment to enable them to cross the River Severn. Here, a Class 118 DMU sets out for Hereford with a service from Worcester Shrub Hill. The cars contribute to the date! 17 September 1986.

A further contrast with changing transport styles is provided by this Railhead Treatment Train (RHTT) in the charge of two filthy Colas Rail Class 66s, Nos 66848 and 66846, which is working a circuit between Gloucester and the Marches line via Worcester. These trains operate during the autumn months to clear leaf mould from the tracks to aid adhesion. 13 November 2017.

A view of the 11.22 London Paddington to Great Malvern service with HST cars Nos 43129 and 43145 in charge as it leaves Foregate Street. 13 November 2017.

Seen across the River Severn, a Class 101 Metro-Cammell DMU that dates back to the late 1950s is heading for Great Malvern with a service from Worcester Shrub Hill. The boat in the foreground will no doubt facilitate river trips during the coming days and evenings. 12 July 1981.

This humble Class 150 Sprinter, No. 150104, is nearing journey's end after a 153-mile trip on the 08.23 service from Southampton Central to Great Malvern. A journey from Solent to Severn! 13 November 2017.

Henwick

This is a thriving suburb situated in the bustling St John's area of Worcester, close to the University of Worcester campus. The railway reaches it by way of a 935-yard bridge comprising a series of brick arches, spans and lattice girders from Foregate Street. The station here closed in 1965 but a signal box dating to 1875 remains, protecting a level crossing over Henwick Road. This box is vital to operations at Foregate Street as some trains turn back here; it also forms the division of the two single lines into the city. A turn-back siding has recently been reinstated here, amazingly controlled by a new lower-quadrant semaphore signal.

A street-level view of Henwick signal box as No. 170502 passes with the 11.39 Hereford to Birmingham New Street service on 28 November 2017. The box is reputed to date back to 1875.

The Brush Class 47 diesels date back to 1963 and were introduced to services in the Worcester area in the late 1960s. They eventually supplanted the Hymek diesel-hydraulics on Cotswold line services some ten years later, until they themselves received competition from the English Electric Class 50 locomotives. No. 47416 passes the site of Henwick station with a London Paddington to Hereford train on 19 April 1980. The signal box can just be seen above the rear coach with St Clement's Church visible at the top middle of the picture.

Work is in hand that hopefully will ease operations at Foregate Street as a turn-back siding is being reinstated at Henwick. Most unusually, a traditional semaphore signal has been installed to protect movements. No. 150109 should have worked the 12.39 from Hereford to Birmingham New Street service, but it was late arriving at Foregate Street and turned round short of its intended destination. 28 November 2017.

A Class 117 has just passed Henwick with a Worcester Shrub Hill to Hereford service. The signal in the foreground has recently been replaced by a new LED signal. 9 May 1986.

Newlands East
(126 miles from London Paddington)

A standard block post controlling a level crossing. A halt called Stocks Lane opened here in 1929, which was renamed Newlands East in 1943 with the installation of sidings for military purposes. This closed in 1965. After the war, the sidings assumed a different role with the creation of a permanent way depot specialising in pre-assembled track (continuous welded rail) until 1982. The yard utilised its own shunting loco, normally PWM654, which was built by Ruston Hornsby. After closure, the loco – much sought after by loco spotters – moved to Worcester Shrub Hill. The signal box, dating from 1900, remains.

Roughly halfway between here and Worcester Foregate Street, a GWR branch trailed off to Bromyard and Leominster. This closed in stages until all traffic ceased in 1964.

To commemorate GWR 150, British Rail adopted this Class 117 DMU and repainted it in chocolate and cream livery. Needless to say, it soon gained celebrity status. I was fortunate to record it approaching Newland East with a Worcester Shrub Hill to Hereford service in glorious weather. W51410 is the leading driving car. 2 June 1985.

A view of the 1900-built Newland East signal box. 2 June 1985.

On a glorious summer's day, the unmistakable shape of the Malvern Hills provide a backdrop to English Electric No. 50046 *Ajax* as it approaches Newland East with a Hereford to London Paddington service. The days of loco-hauled services on this route were fast coming to an end and the Class 50s were to be seen for a few more years. 2 June 1985.

Malvern Link
(128 miles from London Paddington)

The various townships of the Malverns magically line the majestic hills so eulogised by Sir Edward Elgar. They can be seen far and wide across the Midland plain. Malvern Link is very much the business side of the townships, spawning such iconic names as the Morgan Motor Company. For the energetic, it also forms the start of a breathtaking walk across those hills. Opened in 1859, the station was an elegant affair, but unfortunately the buildings except the stationmaster's house were swept away in 1970, five years after closure of the goods yard. However, in recently enlightened years, new, stylish station buildings have been erected, which complement surviving ironwork from days past.

Improvements for the travelling public at Malvern Link are evident here as No. 170634 arrives with a Birmingham New Street to Hereford service. These units have helped popularise services over a route that at one time was threatened with cutbacks. 28 February 2015.

Passing the site of the former goods yard at Malvern Link is a Swindon CrossCountry Class 120 DMU and a Class 117 DMU forming a six-coach Worcester Shrub Hill to Hereford service. 5 February 1977.

The withdrawal of the popular Class 52 Western diesel-hydraulics saw a spate of very popular and usually fully booked charter trains organised during their final months in service. The Monmouthshire Railway Society sponsored this Capital United Express, which is seen speeding through Malvern Link on a route from London Paddington, taking in both Hereford and Worcester, behind D1023 *Western Fusilier*. 5 February 1977.

Great Malvern
(129 miles from London Paddington)

There can be few stations in this country so befitting of the town or city that it serves (York, Glasgow Central and Bristol Temple Meads immediately spring to mind). It is no so much the scale but the style that hits you when you first alight at this station constructed in Victorian Gothic manner by architect E. W. Elmsie in 1861. Its design must be unique, right down to it being embellished with stone carvings, cast-iron brackets and even spandrels in the form of iron foliage. It is a visual delight. Such delights greet you at every turn and it must have been a tragedy when fire sought to take this magnificent station from us in 1986. Fortunately, apart from the clock tower, it survives.

Such is the quirkiness of the place that a separate entrance was constructed to gain access to the adjoining hotel (now a girls' college), which was nicknamed 'The Worm' due to its shape. It is no longer in use. The Up platform buildings are used by a number of small businesses, but the star is the award-winning tearoom, named after a local landowner and Lady of the Manor, Lady Foley. I apologise for the whim in declaring it the 'icing on the cake' for would-be travellers and visitors to the station.

The station itself, in typical GWR fashion, is a little distance from the town that it purports to serve. However, this is understandable given the geographical constraints provided by the hills. Apart from the loss of the clock tower, at first glance the station appears to be intact. However, a third platform was at one time used by Midland Railway services to Ashchurch and Tewkesbury.

A buoyant mixture of services are available from Great Malvern, with a number terminating here.

Destinations are similar to those available at Foregate Street, with perhaps the longest through service being the daily 215-mile jaunt to Brighton!

I make no apology for my enthusiasm over a station very much in keeping with its surroundings and the tranquility afforded to traveller and casual visitor alike.

The Malverns can be one of the first places to experience snow in the Midlands. No. 170631 arrives at Great Malvern with a Birmingham New Street to Hereford service. 7 January 2010.

The end of steam on Hereford services in the mid-1960s saw the introduction of the chunky Hymek Class 35 diesel-hydraulic locomotives. Despite their popularity, hydraulic transmission was not favourable and their tenure lasted less than ten years. Introduced in 1961, the class contained 101 locos, and one example, D7026, is seen with three coaches at Great Malvern on a service from London Paddington to Hereford. It had at one time been the practice to detach the buffet car and other coaches at Worcester Shrub Hill. I can vouch that a ride behind one of these locos with three coaches in tow was a lively experience. 24 March 1973.

A summer 1995 scene of Brush Mirrlees No. 60054 *Charles Babbage* passing through Great Malvern with a diverted Round Oak to Margam empty steel train.

Great Western Railway operates a range of services to Great Malvern. Network Turbo Express No. 166216 has worked over the Cotswold line from London Paddington before terminating here. 28 February 2015.

A First Great Western service in the charge of No. 158958 is seen waiting to leave with the 10.48 to Brighton, a journey of some 215 miles taking in Bristol, Salisbury and Chichester. 12 May 2012.

A winter's morning portrait of Great Malvern station, which sums up its elegance. 16 January 2018.

GWR is undergoing a revolution, electrifying routes and introducing new motive power. This new bi-mode Hitachi IET, No. 800012, was built in Italy, and is seemingly out of place in the 1861-built Great Malvern station, where it has just arrived on the 06.52 from London Paddington. 16 January 2018.

Malvern Wells

(130 miles from London Paddington)

Just under a mile from Great Malvern (GM) lies the signal box at Malvern Wells. Dating back to 1919, it controls movements from GM for terminating trains that have access to a loop before the box and for the tokenless 6-mile block section to Ledbury, which contains two tunnels. The line at this stage is dwarfed by the bulk of North Hill (1,394 feet) before it descends into the narrow single-line bore (1,586 yards) of Colwall Tunnel. This is the second tunnel, the first having been constructed in 1861, but which was found to be too small when new rolling stock was introduced in the 1920s. The present one opened in 1926. Malvern Wells station closed in 1965.

Semaphore signals operated from Malvern Wells control the passage of the 08.21 from London Paddington to Hereford service, which is seen in the charge of HST power cars Nos 43188 and 43196. The well-used loop is evident, and since this image was recorded the tall signal has been replaced by a smaller version. 28 February 2015.

A view looking towards the signal box. Units Nos 172214 and 172221 have just arrived on the 09.46 London Midland Trains service from Dorridge, and will now gain the Up track to run back to Great Malvern to form the 11.35 train to Whitlocks End via Birmingham Snow Hill. 28 February 2015.

A hazy midsummer's day with a six-car DMU bound for Hereford about to enter Colwall Tunnel. Viewed from Lower Wyche, the route of the old Midland Railway branch to Ashchurch can be seen in the middle of the picture, above the golf course. 17 June 1972.

A brief trip over the border into Herefordshire sees a Class 118 DMU enter Colwall Tunnel with a Hereford to Worcester Shrub Hill working. The route into the original tunnel can still be seen to the far right of the train. 24 March 1973.

Colwall

(132 miles from London Paddington)

While not in Worcestershire, I have included Colwall to give an idea of the terrain on the other side of Colwall Tunnel. Opened in 1861, this now single-platformed station is a pleasant start/finish point for walkers across the Malvern Hills.

A glorious spring evening welcomes this Class 119 DMU after it has left the gloom of Colwall Tunnel with an Oxford to Hereford service. These particular units possessed mini buffets, which were removed to create additional luggage space when working services near Heathrow Airport. New trackwork is also evident. 17 April 1984.

The entrance to the single-line Colwall Tunnel can be seen as English Electric No. 50015 *Valiant* bursts into the late summer sunshine with a London Paddington to Hereford service. The Class 50s were named after warships and jointly operated these services into the 1980s with the Brush Class 47s after the demise of the Hymeks. 1 September 1979.

The beauty of the Malvern Hills is captured in this autumn view of No. 50036 *Victorious* thumping away from Colwall with a London Paddington to Hereford service. The house obviously predates the railway and one wonders if any compensation was received for the loss of part of the side wall! 30 September 1981.

The beauty of the Malvern Hills is now transformed by the snow. HST power car No. 43088 leads a London Paddington to Hereford service into Colwall station. Somebody is to be congratulated on clearing the platform edges. 7 January 2010.

Bound for Hereford is Hymek D7037, which, having arrived from London Paddington, stands at the single platform at Colwall. 17 June 1972.

Lowesmoor (Worcester)

Two single lines traverse an embankment between Worcester Foregate Street and Worcester Shrub Hill stations, crossing a distinctive canal bridge over the Worcester & Birmingham Canal at Lowesmoor.

Between the stations at Foregate Street and Shrub Hill, the railway crosses the Worcester & Birmingham Canal by way of a distinctive bridge at Lowesmoor. Now transferred to Hull Trains, Adelante No. 180104 crosses the canal with the 12.06 service from Foregate Street to London Paddington. 13 December 2017.

Above: Brush Class 47 No. 47230 crosses Lowesmoor Bridge with a Paddington to Hereford service. 23 January 1974.

Right: A Tyseley-based Class 116 DMU heads for Worcester Shrub Hill with a service from Great Malvern. 12 July 1981.

Worcester Shrub Hill
(120 miles from London Paddington)

Though a mere shadow of its former self, Shrub Hill has managed to retain a certain air of its former importance. Since the passage of its first trains in 1850, when the OWWR, courtesy of a branch from the nearby Birmingham & Gloucester Railway, entered the city on a route destined for the Black Country, it has been the principal rail centre in the region. The history of the OWWR is intriguing and well worth a read.

Shrub Hill station was surrounded by a network of motive power depots, works, good yards and a labyrinth of lines, including the famous 'Vinegar Branch'. Such installations have disappeared or reduced in status over the years, with the works closing in 1964 and the motive power depot to steam in 1965. Diesels continued to be stabled in rapidly deteriorating conditions until 1973, although in recent years multiple unit-serving facilities have been developed and improved upon.

Resignalling of the area was planned for in 1972, and while certain work was undertaken, traditional signalling methods prevail and add to the charm of the network. Interestingly, 2018 has seen brand-new Hitachi IEP trains being controlled by semaphore signalling!

While Foregate Street is the busier of the two stations passenger-wise, Shrub Hill is the operational centre, with train crews and roster offices being based here. However, it remains to be seen what impact the new Parkway development has on both stations – hopefully, an increase in usage.

In the meantime, we continue to enjoy a station that exudes an atmosphere that goes back fifty years.

Work being undertaken in the Bromsgrove area saw a number of diverted services through Worcester in 2016. This CrossCountry 06.03 Glasgow Central to Plymouth service with power car No. 43285 leading eases through Shrub Hill on 2 November 2016. The station once supported an overall roof and the retaining walls can be seen clearly here.

Worcester will always be associated with the Hymek diesel-hydraulics, although freight workings with them were unusual. The first member of the class, D7000, which was introduced into traffic in 1961, is seen easing a short freight train from the Droitwich Spa direction on the goods-avoiding line on 19 April 1973. Three months later it was withdrawn from service.

D7018 eases onto the stock of a London Paddington train on 10 March 1973. This engine was one of a handful that survived past their planned withdrawal date until March 1975. It is now based on the West Somerset Railway at Williton.

D7030 has just arrived from Hereford with coaches for London Paddington. Further coaches will be attached here. While still being used on top link duties, the loco will be withdrawn two months later. 24 March 1973.

The Western Class 52s had two weeks left in service and Shrub Hill sees D1023 *Western Fusilier* arriving on F&W Tours' 'Western Finale' railtour, which ran from Exeter St Davids to York. A collision with a herd of heifers at Charfield caused damage to an air pipe, which was repaired by a rather inspired Gloucester fitter, apparently with a 10p piece. The DMU is a Class 120 Swindon CrossCountry unit.

Thirty-seven years on and changes, while apparent, are not dramatic. HST power car No. 43177 *Newton Abbot 150* propels the 07.10 service from Hereford to London Paddington away from the station. London Midland Trains No. 172215 is also seen, waiting to depart with the 08.15 to Dorridge. 13 April 2014.

D7022 arrives at Shrub Hill from London Paddington on 22 July 1972. It survived until March 1975.

Past memories of CrossCountry services that actually served Shrub Hill, with Class 45 D121 passing with a Newcastle to Plymouth working. Take note of changes to the trackwork. 22 July 1972.

Due to engineering work at Banbury, No. 47609 provides the power for a diverted Manchester Piccadilly to Poole service on 6 April 1985.

A view from the platform end on 16 June 1973 of the remains of the engine shed. What's left still serves some purpose, with Brush Class 31 D5692 and Hymek Class 35 D7001 keeping a Class 119 DMU company. Shrub Hill Junction signal box, seen here, closed in November 1973 during a remodelling of the layout.

A later view in August 1987 sees a dramatic change to the shed, which affords no shelter for the Network SouthEast-liveried Class 117 DMU.

The English Electric Class 50s became popular on the Cotswold line after seeing duty on West of England services. No. 50003 *Temeraire* waits at the end of Platform 1, looking towards Shrub Hill station signal box on 30 September 1981.

No. 50031 *Hood* is at the same position nearly five years later on 9 May 1986. Happily, *Hood* has been saved by the Fifty Fund.

Formerly situated at the rail depot at Newland, No. 97654 – built by Ruston Hornsby of Lincoln in 1959, and now preserved by the Heritage Shunters Trust at Rowsley – is seen adjacent to Shrub Hill station. 26 February 1986.

A more traditional role was undertaken by No. 08836, which was built in 1959. It would have been used at Shrub Hill as a station pilot, attaching and detaching coaches and parcels vans. The latter would have been substantial due to the existence of a local mail-order warehouse. 22 August 1986.

Diesel power started to oust steam in the Worcester area, initially using DMUs on branch and secondary services. Their popularity was varied but there was no doubt that the ability for passengers to see out of the front windows carried some favour. Network SouthEast adorned their sets with a striking colour scheme, as with this Class 117, which is seen leaving Shrub Hill for Hereford past the iconic signal gantry. 19 September 1986.

Built under the reign of Sir Nigel Gresley, A4 Pacific No. 60009 *Union of South Africa* is privately owned and due to be permanently withdrawn in 2019. It attracts great attention as it arrives at Shrub Hill with the Railway Touring Company's 'Cotswold Venturer' from London Paddington on 26 August 2017. The signal above the engine's boiler will be replaced by a new semaphore, the post of which is adjacent to the fourth coach. This is in readiness for an extension of Platform 1 that will be made to accommodate new IEP trains that are being introduced onto the Cotswold line.

Britannia Class loco No. 70013 *Oliver Cromwell* survived until the end of regular steam working on British Rail and was involved in the final trains in August 1968. It was subsequently preserved and has been a regular performer on the main line. It is seen arriving at Shrub Hill with the return stock of the 'Cathedrals Express' to London Victoria. 16 July 2009.

This Tyseley-based Class 116 DMU is seen arriving at Shrub Hill with a Birmingham New Street to Great Malvern service. The tail lamp has already been added as the train will reverse here. 22 August 1976.

Snow hits the region and the railway continues to operate. A London Paddington to Great Malvern service curves past Shrub Hill Junction, being worked by HST power cars Nos 43128 and 43034. 7 January 2010.

On loan to First Great Western from South West Trains, No. 158887 forms a late-running Great Malvern to Brighton service, while No. 150007 waits in the middle road for its next turn of duty, which will take it to Dorridge. 9 January 2010.

I make no apology for including images featuring the signals at the shed end of Shrub Hill. How much longer they will survive remains open to speculation. There have been piecemeal alterations to signalling thus far, involving replacing old signals with not only LED signals, but also semaphores. Of note here is what is referred to as a 'cash register' signal, which stands to the right of the gantry. It is a space-saving signal, which when pulled off shows which route is set. Originally three routes were available: namely, Hereford, Birmingham or Shed. The latter is no longer available. The image on page 47 shows this quite clearly. Here, a private charter from Tyseley to Gloucester hauled by Castle Class No. 5043 *Earl of Mount Edgcumbe* is seen as it approaches the station. 9 January 2010.

The popular English Electric Class 37s continue to be seen on a variety of workings in the Worcester area. They were originally based here for banking duties on the Lickey Incline. Colas Rail No. 37219 disturbs the peace of Shrub Hill as it works a test train from Bristol to Derby, tailed by No. 37254. 11 August 2016.

Privately owned No. 37057 is being operated by Colas Rail on this Derby to Cardiff test train, which it is seen propelling through Platform 2 at Shrub Hill. The bridge and lift are both derelict and could be real assets to the station. 15 August 2016.

Newly overhauled (rebuilt) No. 37424 in the guise of No. 37558, owned by Direct Rail Services, heads what appears to be a 'jolly' for staff on coach *Caroline* from Ealing Broadway to Reading via Severn Tunnel Junction. At least two of the participants appear keen to record their passage past the signals at Shrub Hill. 14 December 2016.

Freight traffic is sparse, but with passenger services occupying the two through platforms at Shrub Hill for long periods, there are occasions when such services can be diverted round the back road on the goods lines. I was fooled on 10 July 2015 when No. 60092 headed its Round Oak to Margam empty steels around the back.

Rail Operations Group Brush No. 47812 also went 'back road' on its way to collect stock from Long Marston. 13 June 2017.

Diesel charter trains can often be seen calling at or passing Shrub Hill. DRS Nos 37601 and 37603 are in charge of a Pathfinders Tour from Crewe to Kingswear when seen here on 29 August 2014.

In the early morning of 25 June 2010, a Northern Belle luxury train calls at Shrub Hill behind DBS Nos 67002 and 67018. Originally intended for a variety of purposes, these locos are consigned to occasional charter work and spot hire following the demise of postal traffic.

Those signals once again witness the passage of yet another charter hauled by DRS No. 57301 and tailed by No. 57310 on a Chester Model Railway Club/Ffestiniog Railway 'The Great Western Express' railtour, which ran from Hooton to Oxford. 11 April 2015.

This new Hitachi bi-mode train, No. 800015, looks out of place among the steam-age infrastructure at Shrub Hill as it arrives on a murky day with the 12.02 service from Worcester Foregate Street to London Paddington. 13 February 2018.

A railtour that didn't quite go to plan was Vintage Trains' double pannier tank tour around parts of the West Midlands. Pannier tank No. 9600 failed on the outward leg and Brush No. 47773 was used to assist Hawksworth pannier No. 9466 for the remainder of the tour. The revised pairing are seen arriving at Shrub Hill. 12 November 2016.

A new signal has been erected at Shrub Hill in connection with the extension of Platform 1. Turbo No. 166202 runs into Platform 2 to form a service to London Paddington, which should have started at Hereford. Shrub Hill station signal box dates back to 1935. 5 October 2017.

The 10.22 London Paddington to Hereford service arrives at Shrub Hill with HST power car No. 43146 leading. It seems strange to believe that most of the infrastructure here might outlive the train. 15 August 2017.

This image captures the atmosphere to be enjoyed at Shrub Hill during certain times of the day. Driver and guard make their way to their train as despatch staff wait anxiously to send the 13.17 to Dorridge on its way. No. 172338 is the unit. 23 March 2017.

The ornate building on Platform 2 was formerly the ladies waiting room and reputedly moved from the original Worcester station at Spetchley. It is understood that it qualified as the first portable building in Europe. 10 July 2015.

Earlier days at Shrub Hill. Sulzer Class 25 No. 25195 has an easy job with just one parcels van, which is bound for Lawley Street in Birmingham. Such traffic was considerable here with much business generated from the Kay & Cos mail-order warehouse. Sadly, if such traffic is still in existence it has been lost to the roads. 6 April 1985.

A footpath known as Railway Walk would afford good views over the railway complex at Worcester. Unfortunately, these views would be of a vastly changing railway given the rationalisation over the last fifty years. The view is very much screened by foliage these days. Brush Class 31 No. 31301 approaches Tunnel Junction where the Shrub Hill and Foregate Street lines diverge with a parcels van for Lawley Street in Birmingham. Cast your eyes beyond the train and imagine a vast area of goods sidings, locomotive depots and works. A glimpse of Shrub Hill station can be seen in the top right-hand corner. The diesel servicing depot is now situated to the right of the semaphore signals. 6 October 1984.

Another view from Railway Walk sees English Electric Class 37s Nos 37158 and 37271 in the holding sidings adjacent to Tunnel Junction on 6 October 1984. Worcester Tunnel Junction signal box continues to control movements here.

Tunnel Junction and Rainbow Hill

A standard ex-GWR signal box dating back to 1905 controls movements into both Worcester stations from the Droitwich Spa direction in addition to the freight and loco depot routes. In the Droitwich direction is Rainbow Hill Tunnel; on the opposite side is a splendid gantry signal that controls incoming trains to Worcester.

The 212-yard-long Rainbow Hill Tunnel is to be found in the Droitwich direction. A Class 118 DMU makes a smoky exit with a Great Malvern to Birmingham New Street service on 6 July 1980. The distinctive signal gantry remains to this day, controlling the route to Foregate Street to the right, Shrub Hill to the centre and the goods loop to the left.

Another Great Malvern to Birmingham New Street service this time in the hands of Swindon-built Class 120 CrossCountry DMU leaves Rainbow Hill Tunnel. In the foreground is a limit of shunt indicator. 22 August 1976.

In the days when cross-country InterCity trains called at Worcester Shrub Hill (lengthening their schedules by around twenty minutes), No. 47244 approaches Rainbow Hill Tunnel with the 09.15 Birmingham New Street to Taunton train. To the rear of the train is the site of an unadvertised halt used by munitions workers in the two world wars. 29 May 1978.

Another cross-country service with Sulzer Class 45 No. 45051 in charge leaves Rainbow Hill Tunnel on 22 August 1981.

Celebrity visitors to the area are always popular, not to mention the iconic locomotives that used to grace the East Coast Main Line. Deltic No. 55022 *Royal Scots Grey* exits Rainbow Hill with Pathfinder Tours' *Heart of Wales Explorer*, which will see the Class 55 cover a route from Cardiff Central through Central Wales to Crewe. 29 March 2008.

Just under a month later we see one of the Deltics' predecessors, A4 Pacific No. 60019 *Bittern*, making just as impressive an exit from Rainbow Hill Tunnel with Kingfisher Railtours' 'The Severn Valley Phoenix', which ran from Kensington Olympia to Kidderminster. 19 April 2008.

Two years later and another railtour taking in the Severn Valley Railway emerges from the tunnel in the form of preserved Hastings DEMU set No. 1001 with the 'Severn Explorer', running from Hastings to Bridgnorth. Unfortunately, this viewpoint has been taken away from us following a number of antisocial incidents in the area. Tunnel Junction signal box can just be seen at the far end of the tunnel. 24 April 2010.

Droitwich Spa
(126 miles from London Paddington)

North from Worcester is Droitwich Spa, which was at one time famous for the healing qualities of its brine baths. It is now very much a commuter town for workers in Birmingham, the West Midlands and Worcester. The standard two-platformed station provides a good service to these destinations.

Droitwich Spa is also the junction for routes to Birmingham New Street via Bromsgrove and the old OWWR route into Birmingham Snow Hill via Stourbridge Junction and the Black Country. The lines diverge near the site of the former goods and coal yards, and once again are controlled by semaphore signalling under the jurisdiction of the 1907-built box. There is a good selection of semaphore signals here, including a distinctive starter signal on the Birmingham platform. The Bromsgrove route was singled in the 1970s, making operations difficult, an example of which is shown later.

The Malvern Hills can still be spotted in the background of this image of Brush Class 31 No. 31403 approaching Droitwich Spa with a diverted London Paddington to Birmingham New Street service. Engineering work in the Banbury area caused several such workings to be routed via the Cotswold line. 6 April 1985.

Colas Rail Brush locos Nos 47727 and 47739 approach Droitwich Spa with a movement of wagons from Long Marston to Chaddesden on 16 June 2010.

Super power for General Manager's saloon *Caroline* in the form of DRS Class 37s Nos 37423 and 37409, which are seen passing the distinctive starter signals at Droitwich Spa. The latter loco appears to be fresh from the works. The pair are routed via Bromsgrove. 16 June 2010.

The Western Locomotive Association's superb Class 52 D1015 *Western Champion* swings off the Kidderminster route at Droitwich Spa on the Bescot to Weymouth leg of a Pathfinder Tours railtour from Leicester. Semaphore signals control this busy junction. The signal box dates to 1907. 7 September 2013.

A scene depicting a bygone age, when goods yards still existed and pick-up freights served them. Droitwich Spa by now had only a coal yard owned by Underwoods, who still maintained a private shunting locomotive. Brush Class 31 No. 31231 shunts a coal train from Bescot in between the passage of passenger trains. 3 October 1977.

Diverted via Bromsgrove and under stormy skies is this Manchester Piccadilly to London Paddington service, which will take the Cotswold line. It is headed by Class 50 No. 50042 *Superb*. The coal yard still appears to be doing good business. 6 April 1985.

Droitwich sees a number of workings bound for Long Marston, which has built up an engineering and storage base for rail vehicles. Rail Operation Group No. 37884 is seen hauling some Class 319 EMUs from Bedford that are bound for storage. Note the special coupling equipment necessary to enable the loco to tow such units. 30 August 2017.

The coal yard has disappeared and comparisons can be made with earlier pictures as Castle Class loco No. 5043 *Earl of Mount Edgcumbe* pulls away from a water stop at Droitwich Spa with a Vintage Trains circular tour from Tyseley to Hereford. 25 March 2017.

Above: Disaster has struck No. 47628 at Droitwich Spa. The locomotive failed in the station, blocking the junction on a day of diverted traffic. It was working a Poole to Manchester Piccadilly service. The consist managed to limp across the junction but still blocked the Bromsgrove route. Assistance was sent for in the form of two Class 37 locos that were assigned to banking duties on the Lickey Incline, but they had to come from Gloucester. 6 April 1985.

Right: A helping shove from two banking engines, Nos 37222 and 37224, as they attempt to rescue No. 47628. I am not sure what happened later, but I can only imagine the noise as the two engines assisted the train up the Lickey! 6 April 1985.

Hartlebury
(132 miles from London Paddington)

At first glance this is a rather anonymous roadside station serving the distant village of Hartlebury.

At one time Hartlebury Castle was home of the Bishop of Worcester, while a nearby factory estate housed Second World War aeroplane spares. Dating back to 1852, the station was at one time a junction for the Severn Valley Railway, but that function ceased in 1970 with the closure of the section to Bewdley via Stourport-on-Severn. The signal box, which dated back to 1876, unfortunately closed in 2012.

Until recently train services here were sparse, but have thankfully increased partly due to the establishment of an excellent brewery and brewery tap in the main station building.

The penultimate day for Hartlebury signal box, which dated back to 1876. No. 172211 heads for Dorridge. 23 August 2012.

A convoy of diesels bound for an open day commemorating Old Oak Common motive power depot pass Hartlebury from the Severn Valley Railway at Kidderminster. Western Class D1015, Class 50s Nos 50035, 50044, and locos D407 and No. 50049 are seen on 30 August 2017.

Another view of the convoy. Such sights are not unusual given the close proximity of the Severn Valley Railway and the need often for other railways to borrow guest locomotives. 30 August 2017.

Kidderminster
(135 miles from London Paddington)

Traditionally a town famous for its manufacture of carpets, Kidderminster is perhaps more famous now as the home of Kidderminster Harriers AFC, as well as the terminus of the Severn Valley Railway. Upon approaching the town from the south, the growth of the preserved railway is evident and indicative of its effect on passenger usage on the main line. Very much a commuter town, the people of Kidderminster have deserved better facilities than those provided by the existing station. The Severn Valley Railway throws it into shame. However, improvements are promised.

West Midlands Trains and Chiltern Railways cater for the needs of in excess of one and a half million passengers annually, with services to Stratford-upon-Avon, Great Malvern, Birmingham Moor Street and Snow Hill, as well as peak-hour through services to London Marylebone.

Celebrity Class 117 DMU No. 117305 was used in the West Midlands on 5 May 1986, working services from Kidderminster to Birmingham New Street in conjunction with a Midline festival. There were some doubts over its reliability and a Class 128 parcels car was attached to ensure that it had sufficient power to enable it to ascend Old Hill bank. Note the Severn Valley Railway adjacent to this image.

A celebrity visitor brought in by Midline was English Electric Class 40 D213 *Andania*. This loco is now certified for main-line running and can be seen on the East Lancashire Railway. 5 May 1986.

Kidderminster station is inadequate for its present usage and improvements have been mooted. Class 150 Sprinter No. 150104 forms a Dorridge train on 1 May 2010.

Kidderminster has been re-signalled since this view of No. 66119 passing through with a Margam to Round Oak steel train on 10 September 2009. The buildings to the right are occupied by the Severn Valley Railway.

Blakedown and Hagley

The last two stations before entering what is now the West Midlands are at Stourbridge. Both serve Worcestershire commuter villages and each station carries its own identity. Blakedown was originally known as Churchill & Blakedown. The signal box opened in 1888, was closed in 2012, and has subsequently been donated by Network Rail to the parish council for use as a local amenity. It has been moved away from the track but remains close to the station. The station has two platforms but rather spartan shelter.

Hagley retains a well-maintained building, with a booking office and classic footbridge dating back to 1884, which Hornby used as a basis for one of its models. It is now Grade II listed.

South of Blakedown, these two ex-GWR pannier tanks were recorded on a Vintage Trains tour of the West Midlands, taking in Stratford-upon-Avon and Worcester. The locos are Nos 9600 and 7752. 4 November 2012.

Passing Churchill & Blakedown signal box are West Coast Railways Nos 47854 and 47804, which are seen hauling the first leg of the Severn Valley Limited to York on 14 March 2009.

Blakedown station has little to commend itself these days, but at least the presence of a former GWR running board helps to make it look presentable. No. 60044 *Dowlow* is given a run out on a Round Oak to Margam empty steels train after several weeks of shunting duties at Bescot yard. 7 October 2015.

Hagley station retains a certain GWR atmosphere about it, with its vintage bridge and booking office. No. 60040 *The Territorial Army Centenary* attracts attention while passing through with a Round Oak to Margam empty steel train. 14 May 2014.

The Class 172 DMUs have transformed services on lines radiating from Birmingham Snow Hill. Seen here calling at Hagley, No. 172215 is the leading unit of a Dorridge to Worcester Foregate train. 29 May 2012.

Bromsgrove, Barnt Green and Redditch

Bromsgrove, a town once associated with the woollen trade, joined the railway map in 1840 when the Birmingham & Gloucester Railway entered the town. It is famous for being at the bottom of the infamous Lickey Incline, which at 1 in 37 remains the steepest continuous main-line climb in the country. At one time a considerable number of banking engines were maintained at Bromsgrove for the purpose of assisting both freight and passenger trains towards Birmingham. That practice has dwindled with the advent of modern, lighter trains and fewer freight workings. Additionally, Bromsgrove has benefitted from a new station, which should shortly see a vastly improved service.

Barnt Green, just over the brow of the incline, is the last station before the West Midlands. A well-heeled commuter village at the foot of the Lickey Hills should see its function as a junction station for the Redditch branch enhanced with additional services to and from Bromsgrove.

Redditch, famous for needle manufacturing, road roundabouts and as an overspill town for Birmingham, lies at the southern end of the CrossCity line that stretches from Lichfield, through Birmingham, and into Worcestershire. Its railways have seen upward improvements since the closure of a through route taking in Evesham and Ashchurch in 1963. Incorporated into CrossCity services since 1990, they are unrecognisable since those Cinderella days.

This view of Bromsgrove has been transformed following the construction of a new station.
The sidings to the left were used by banking locos on Lickey Incline duties. Freightliners Nos 66523 and 66559 on an empty coal train bound for Avonmouth drift into the loop to allow a passenger train to overtake. 8 April 2010.

'The Great Britain' is a prestigious steam tour of the country and visits various locations. With Black Five No. 44871 and Britannia Class No. 70013 *Oliver Cromwell* in charge, the tour accelerates towards the Lickey Incline at Bromsgrove. 8 April 2010.

Providing back-up to the steam tour are Western Class 52 D1015 *Western Champion* and West Coast Railways No. 47760, which are seen shortly after the tour has passed by. 8 April 2010.

After the end of steam, there was a reduced requirement for banking engines at Bromsgrove. Nevertheless, it was still possible to see Hymek Class 35s on duty. Here, D7100 and D7001 wait for their next 'push'! 22 July 1972.

A Tyseley 'hybrid' DMU containing a Metro-Cammell Class 101 driving trailer suffered a failure in Bromsgrove station with a Great Malvern to Birmingham New Street service. Fortunately, Nos 37295 and 37227 were available to lend assistance. Here, the consist attacks the 2-mile incline. 6 October 1979.

Nearing the top of the incline, and passing Vigo, is No. 60068, which is seen working a heavy Margam to Corby loaded steel coil train. It is assisted by No. 66058. These days any banking assistance is sent by way of a dedicated locomotive from Saltley. 11 October 2007.

Another view of the final push up the Lickey by No. 66058. 11 October 2007.

A popular train to view on the Lickey used to be the empty tanks from Westerleigh to Lindsey, which were usually hauled by a Class 60 locomotive. Changing traffic flows means that this lengthy train no longer runs. In happier days, No. 60096 ascends the bank with this working. 11 February 2010.

The Lickey Incline is breasted at Blackwell, where relief loops are available. This was an unusual tour; organised by F. & W. Tours using just three coaches on a Worcester to Tintern circuit, it was hauled by English Electric Class 20 loco No. 20098. The participants seemed happy and I can well remember the anticipation of its arrival given the noise it generated on the incline. 13 August 1978.

Above: A classic working on the Birmingham to Bristol main line in the form of Sulzer No. 45015, which is seen approaching Blackwell while working a Newcastle to Bristol train. 13 August 1978.

Right: Another view of the Westerleigh to Lindsey empty tanks approaching a snowy Barnt Green behind No. 60015. 24 January 2013.

Snow greets this Class 122 unit at Barnt Green on a New Year's Day Saturday lunchtime service from Redditch to Birmingham New Street. Services at this time were sparse and the future looked bad until the CrossCity line was created. 1 January 1977.

Sulzer No. 45008 rattles across the junction at Barnt Green with a cross-country service from Newcastle to Bristol Temple Meads. Barnt Green remains a bleak station, even taking into account a vastly improved passenger service. 1 January 1977.

Right: During the early 1970s, freight traffic to Redditch in the form of stone workings resumed. This was in connection with the reconstruction of the town centre. Sulzer Class 25s D7630 and D7536 hammer their way through the branch platforms at Barnt Green with an empty working on 26 May 1973.

Below: Heard approaching for many minutes, Colas Rail No. 37421 and tailing Network Rail No. 97301 disturb the peace at Barnt Green as they run onto the electrified section with a returning test train from Barnstaple to Derby. 10 February 2016.

The Rail Operations Group use UK Rail Leasing's Brush Nos 56104 and 56098 to move a Railvac machine from Long Marston to Doncaster through Barnt Green. 6 February 2017.

Times have changed on the Redditch branch; now the end of the line is more or less integrated with the bus station and shopping centre, and the station is a simple affair. Services are regular and patronage is buoyant. No. 323208 waits to return as the 11.27 to Lichfield Trent Valley on 16 March 2012.

Class 122 DMU M55004 is sufficient to cater for this Saturday lunchtime train to Birmingham New Street. It is photographed as it prepares to leave the basic platform at Redditch on 27 August 1977. Tyseley had an allocation of these single-car units for use on services at Stourbridge Town, Stratford-upon-Avon and the Redditch branch.

Worcester Wylds Lane and Norton Junction

Heading east from Worcester Shrub Hill, it will be noted that there is considerable residential development taking place on former railway land. Lea & Perrins, famous for its excellent Worcestershire Sauce, can be seen to the right, while the former rail-connected works of the Metal Box Company is to the left.

Norton Junction lies around 3 miles from Shrub Hill and sees the divergence of the old Midland Railway route towards Cheltenham Spa via Abbotswood Junction. To our left is the single line of the Cotswold main line through to Evesham and Oxford. Norton Junction signal box dates back to 1908 and controls a handful of semaphore signals, although there has been an intrusion of LED signals.

Wylds Lane, Worcester, overlooks the Metal Box Company, which as can be seen was once rail-connected. The view from what is Perry Wood Walk gives an expansive view of the layout to the east of Shrub Hill station, as well as Wylds Lane signal box, which closed in 1973. Hymek D7091 has just left Shrub Hill with a service for London Paddington when seen on 22 July 1972.

A later view over Wylds Lane captures No. 50012 *Benbow* shortly after leaving Worcester Shrub Hill for London Paddington. 22 August 1981.

Norton Junction is where the Cotswold main line strikes off to the left and crosses the Midland main line. The connection to this line can be seen trailing off to the right. Brush No. 47466 comes off the Cotswold line with a service from London Paddington to Worcester Shrub Hill when captured on 19 April 1980. Norton Junction box dates back to 1908.

With the Cotswold line bridge in the background, Sulzer No. 46016 hammers west towards Cheltenham Spa with a cross-country express. This area is in the process of being transformed by the new Worcester Parkway station. 19 April 1980.

Pershore

Pershore station is 1 mile from the town that it serves, and is actually located in the village of Pinvin. Opened in 1852, it is an ordinary one-platformed affair that has a surprisingly good service on the Cotswold main line. Between here and Evesham, the line passes some of the most fertile and arable land in the UK.

Central Trains and Thames Trains jointly celebrated the 150th anniversary of the opening of the line between Stourbridge and Evesham on 5 May 2002 and a special train travelled between the two points. At Pershore station, television personality and local resident Alistair McGowan unveiled a new enamel station name board to commemorate the event.

Passing Lower Moor between Pershore and Evesham, HST power car No. 43024 heads the 10.17 London Paddington to Hereford service on 26 November 2017.

Evesham
(86 miles from London Paddington)

The present Evesham station was opened by the OWWR in 1852 and was incorporated into the GWR in 1863. The Midland Railway opened its station in 1864 on a through route between Barnt Green and Ashchurch via Redditch. That closed in 1963 and apart from a few distinctive buildings its site has since been developed. Recent developments have seen a redoubling of the Cotswold line towards Moreton-in-Marsh, but westwards to Norton Junction the route remains single. While the 1957-built signal box remains, it no longer controls any semaphore signals.

Happy memories of Evesham as Hymek D7032 arrives from London Paddington with a train for Worcester Shrub Hill. These sturdy little locos were popular with staff and enthusiasts alike for their fast turn of speed and ability to handle top link express workings on the Western Region main line. 19 April 1973.

The superbly maintained ex-GWR station at Evesham plays host to HST No. 43128 while the loco works the 13.14 Hereford to London Paddington service on 4 February 2015.

A Derby to Oxford Network Rail test train adds a splash of colour to the surroundings at Evesham as it passes through, top and tailed by Colas Rail Nos 37219 and 37175 on 2 December 2015.

A Bristol to Derby test train powers away from Evesham, top and tailed by DRS locos Nos 37612 and 37609 on 21 April 2016. The site of the former Midland Railway station is to the left and the line curved away to Ashchurch to the left after the bridge.

A parcels train from Worcester Shrub Hill to London makes a call at Evesham behind Brush No. 31226. The view from this bridge has changed dramatically, with the construction of new houses and the obligatory supermarket! 19 April 1980.

Above: A February 1980 view of Evesham station, with the site of the old Midland station being cleared to the right. No. 50046 *Ajax* waits to leave with a service from London Paddington to Worcester Shrub Hill.

Right: Regional Railway sprinters were to be seen for a short period on certain Cotswold line services. No. 150268 approaches Evesham with an Oxford to Great Malvern service on 6 May 1989.

Immediately to the east of Evesham station, the railway crosses the River Avon on a girder bridge. No. 47420 crosses with a London Paddington to Worcester Shrub Hill train on 19 April 1980.

It is not unusual to see convoys of locomotives and rolling stock bound for storage, repair or scrap at Long Marston passing Evesham. They usually attract the attention of enthusiasts and I ventured to record the passing of this English Electric convoy, which originated from Barrow Hill and consisted of Nos 20901 and 20905 hauling Nos 37412, 37672 and 37029. 20 March 2009.